Trump and the Iranian Islamists: The Threat to World Peace

Second Edition

Siamak Adibi, MD, PhD

New Publishing Partners
Washington, DC

Published by New Publishing Partners
2510 Virginia Avenue
Suite 902N
Washington, DC 20037
www.npp-publishing.com

ISBN-13: 978-0-9882500-5-5
ISBN-10: 0-9882500-5-5

Second edition

Cover design, book design, and photo editing by Deborah Lange
Back cover photograph by Bill Brine.

Reviews

Siamak Adibi's thoughtful perspective on the Middle East, Iran and the United States is as sensible and refreshing as one could possibly hope for in this troubled world today. His experience as an immigrant and building a distinguished career here makes him a persuasive advocate for humane and constructive approaches to relations between his native country and his American home. Our leaders could benefit greatly from his wisdom.

—Maxwell King
President of The Pittsburgh Foundation

Many Americans are troubled by the decades-long deterioration of U.S.-Iranian relations, but particularly since the Trump administration's withdrawal from the Iran nuclear deal in 2018. Against this backdrop, Dr. Adibi's book is a cry for peace at a time when further deterioration could result in war. The rich anecdotes and photos remind us that relations could be better. What is required is political will from leaders in both Washington and Tehran.

—Professor Ross Harrison
Georgetown University and The University of Pittsburgh

With the U.S. and Iran on the verge of war, Dr. Adibi's book arrived at the right time. Adibi makes a convincing argument that Trump and the Iranian Islamists threaten world peace. The book is a valuable perspective from a distinguished doctor and scholar who knew the Shah of Iran and was briefly appointed Imperial Chief of Medicine. The photos showing the author's early life in Iran are a bonus.

—Professor Emeritus James H. Morris, PhD
Carnegie Mellon University

What I love most about Adibi's book is its clarity—capturing in 49 pages Persian history, the author's childhood and family story, his indomitable spirit and the evolution of Iran-U.S. enmity. I read it in one sitting and felt a closer connection to Dr. Adibi and his wish for world peace.

—*Pamela Meadowcroft Holland, PhD*
Past Co-President of ARCS Foundation Pittsburgh

To my family

If you want to make peace with your enemy, you have to work with your enemy. Then he becomes your partner.

—*Nelson Mandela*

Contents

1. Introduction

When I was a teenager, I read books and essays by French writers. Among the ones I came across were those by the famous French writer Anatole France, who wrote about the horrors of war. His writings terrified me, and I have been thinking about world peace ever since. Over half a century ago, France became known for his crusades for world peace. This led to his election to the French Academy, designed to maintain standards of literary excellence, and receiving the Nobel Prize for Literature in 1921.

A few years ago, I became greatly concerned when I learned that Donald Trump and the Iranian Revolutionary Guard have been threatening to use war to achieve their goals. When the Iranian reformists asked that their Revolutionary Guard stop warfare in the Middle East, the government responded by putting the reformists in prison. As far as Trump is concerned, he has been talking of attacking several countries. Leaders in America and Iran do not seem to be aware of the legacy of Anatole France, his hope, and his preaching for peace among nations.

America has recently become the most prominent warmonger in the world. We have attacked countries like Vietnam, Iraq, Afghanistan, Syria, and North Africa. This has translated into great loss of soldiers and resources, regretfully, without winning any war.

In this book, my intention is to explain my concerns about whether world peace can ever be reached.

2. My Ancestors

I was born in Iran of noble ancestry that goes back to the middle ages. For many centuries, Greek historians referred to the people and the Kings who were living in Iran as Persians. They generalized a small region of Iran known as Pars or Fars. The name Iran was given to the country in 1935 under the first Pahlavi King, the Reza Shah. He was the first ruler who was able to unify the many different ethnic and religious tribes into one country. Today the term Persian connotes the ancient civilization of Persia, and Iranian has come to mean the modern Islamic government of Iran. My family aligns itself more with the designation of Persian.

"Satrap" was the title given to Persians ruling outlying parts of the Persian Empire. One of the earliest Kings, Darius, in order to control his vast empire, came up with a system of appointing members of noble families as a satrapies. The satrapies lived in areas far from the central government. They were loyal to the King in Tehran and were assigned to collect the taxes and keep order.

In the 16th century, Shah Abbas, the great Safavid King, appointed my ancestor Amir Ahmad as a satrap to rule the Caucuses, an area that includes what is known today as Georgia, Armenia, and Azerbaijan. One of my ancestor's assignments was to ensure that the Silk Road in that area remained open and safe for trade. These Persian territories were in danger of being taken over by the Ottoman Emperor and the Czar of Russia.

Unfortunately, the Caucuses were lost to Russia in 1840 and my ancestors had to leave the Caucuses and move to Tehran and join the Ghajar King. Eventually, the Ghajar dynasty grew corrupt and incompetent, causing Persia to fall into chaos and putting it in danger of coming apart. My father, Sadegh Khan, an officer in the Persian Army in the 1920s, became concerned about the survival of the Persian Kingdom. To save Persia, he banded together a small group of brave army officers to overthrow the Ghajar dynasty. On December 12, 1925, the National Senate, known as the Majlis, officially deposed the Ghajar King and declared Reza Khan as Shah. Reza Khan was a brilliant army officer, and he founded the Pahlavi Dynasty. Pahlavi recalls the Middle Persian language of the Sassanian Empire. Reza Khan was born in the Mazandaran Province. His father was a commissioned officer and his mother was a Muslim immigrant from Georgia.

Reza Shah started major projects to rebuild the country. He established many schools and universities. He built railroads, roads, and hospitals. He centralized the government and suppressed tribal rebellions. He prohibited women from wearing the chador because he wanted to bring them out of the Dark Ages and into modernity. In short, he brought the country into the 20th century.

He reinstituted the Parliament and appointed Mohammad Mossadegh as prime minister. My father favored democracy and establishing a constitutional monarchy, and he supported Reza Shah for that reason. But during the 1930s, Reza Shah became a dictator and my father resigned from the army. For more details, see my father's book, *30 Years with the Reza Shah in the Army*.[1]

Reza Shah could not stop the British from taking the Persian oil. He developed business relations with the Germans. In 1941, after World War II broke out, the British became suspicious of the Shah's relationship with Nazi Germany.

Consequently, they deposed Reza Shah and exiled hm to South

---

1   *30 Years with the Reza Shah in the Army*, published in Farsi by Nasar Alborz, Tehran, Iran, in the Persian calendar year 1385 (U.S. calendar year 2006).

Africa. The British then put his son, Mohammad Reza, on the Peacock throne.

3. Pahlavi Dynasty

I got to know the Reza Shah's son, the Crown Prince Mohammad Reza. My family's summer villa was very close to the summer villa of the Pahlavi family, and I would often see him going through our property on his horse. As a result, we got to know each other.

This friendship turned out to be helpful to me when the Crown Prince followed his father to become his Majesty the King.

Mohammad Shah continued the push toward modernization that his father had started. He and his last wife, Farah, did much to emancipate and educate women. They initiated legislation that gave an extended maternity leave and they promoted women into positions of responsibility and power. One of those appointments was given to my sister Faranak who became Minister of Health and then later Cultural Attache to Turkey. The royal couple also did much to restore historic buildings and bring back ancient craftsmanship.

The 1970s were a period of unrest for Iran as the Shah struggled with cancer, and economic and cultural divisions within the country worsened. In 1979, he was forced to abdicate to the Islamic Republic, and thus ended the Pahlavi Dynasty and 2,500 years of the monarchy in Iran.

4. Leaving Iran

In 1950, when I was a teenager, I decided to come to America for my medical education, a step recommended by my teachers. I had to work hard to get my father's approval to go to a country over 12,000 miles away. I persisted with my request, promising my father I would come back every year to see him. Unfortunately, I could not deliver on my promise because schoolwork turned out to be demanding and travel to Iran was expensive. My father died after twelve years of waiting for me come back. For a long time, I carried the sorrow of not being able to deliver on my promise to my father. You can see my father's sadness in the picture of my last night in Tehran before my departure. My sister, brother, and I look cheerful, but my father looks grim.

Before my departure from Iran, I ran into a serious obstacle with the government staff. I needed to exchange my Persian money for American dollars. For this I had to go to the National Bank of Iran. When I got there, the bank president told me that the government had stopped exchanging money because it had a shortage of dollars. I became upset because this would have killed my plan to go to America for my medical education. I decided to fight the government.

I held a meeting in my house with my friends who were planning to go abroad to let them know of my plan to fight the

My last night in Tehran. My sister, brother
and I (on the left) look cheerful, but my father looks grim.

government. They all agreed with my plan, which was a peaceful sitdown strike in the Parliament until the government agreed to exchange our money.

In the late afternoon, when the deputies had gone home, we took over the Chamber of Deputies and planned to sleep there

His Majesty's office in the Royal Palace. The King is in the center
and the King's personal General is behind him. On the left side in a
dark suit, I am standing presenting my problem to the King.

until morning. The King heard of our strike and sent his Chief General, his second in command, to bring me to his office. I was happy to go and took a few selective members of my group with me. As we entered the Royal Palace, we were ushered into His Majesty's office.

The King was happy to see me. He remembered me from the days when he was still the crown prince. He was supportive of our wanting to go abroad for our education because he had done the same himself. He called Prime Minister Mossadegh and convinced him of the importance of our going abroad to get an excellent education. It would be good for us and good for the country.

The next day we were on the front page of the Tehran newspapers for our victory. Shortly afterward, in the early fall of 1950, we headed to the airport to leave Iran.

My team and I leaving the office of the King in the
Royal Palace. I am in front, wearing a black suit.

5. My Experience with the Last Pahlavi King

Several years later, the King honored me with a big prize, inspired by a letter he received from the Iranian ambassador in Washington, D.C. The ambassador wrote him to tell him that I was the best Iranian student in America. The ambassador knew this because he had read my transcript from the Johns Hopkins University in Baltimore, MD. The Shah summoned my father to the Royal Palace to find out what I would like to receive from him as my prize. My father responded that I would like to receive financial support to complete my medical education because it was expensive. The King immediately asked the director of his foundation to cover all of my expenses until I had finished my medical education. I was overwhelmed by the King's generosity, which made my life much easier, as I no longer would have to worry about paying my medical school expenses.

After the King awarded me with financial support, I was able to take care of my debts to Johns Hopkins University for my pre-medical degree and to the Jefferson Medical College in Philadelphia for my medical degree. Jefferson is the second oldest medical school in America. I was also awarded the gold medal of surgery by the Governor of Pennsylvania.

After medical school, I moved to Boston to get post-medical

training in gastroenterology at Harvard hospitals and eventually a PhD degree in the nutritional sciences from MIT in Cambridge. The Shah paid for all my training. By then, I was exhausted from going to all these schools. Fortunately, I was immediately recruited by the University of Pittsburgh School of Medicine to serve as a tenured professor of medicine and to establish a pioneering division of gastroenterology and nutrition.

My reputation as a skilled clinician and productive medical researcher rapidly grew, and I became known nationally and internationally. I was sought after by medical schools in this country and in Europe. I accepted two visiting professorships, one in Germany at the University of Erlangen-Nuremberg and the other in Italy at the University of Bari. This necessitated frequent trips to Europe to give lectures.

During the 1970s the King heard of my accomplishments and became interested in bringing me back to Iran. In consultation with his health minister he invited me to become his Imperial Chief of Medicine. After several days of thinking, I came to the conclusion that in the light of his many generosities toward me, I had no choice but to accept his invitation. So, I flew to Tehran to meet with the King in his palace and to tell him that I was honored to accept his offer. You can see my picture with the King and his health minister.

He seemed pleased by my acceptance and began to tell me of his dream to build an international center of medicine in northern Tehran. The center would be used to treat patients from Iran and other Middle Eastern countries. In fact, he told me that the basis of his dream was to revive the glories of the pre-Islamic Persia. Among the past glories was the creation of the world-renowned International University in Ancient Persia in 27 AC during the 400-year era of the Persian Sassanid Dynasty. That university had a large library containing 400,000 books and a large faculty of international scholars teaching a wide variety of subjects, with medicine being the most prominent one. There was a well-organized medical center, under the direction of a medical director, and a large medical staff including physicians and pharmacists. This was the first of its kind in the world, created a

I am accepting the King's invitation to become Imperial Chief of Medicine. The Minister of Health is standing between the King (on the left) and me.

thousand years ago. I was excited about the King's plan to create such a medical center to remind the Western people of how advanced Persia was in antiquity. I promised the King that I would make every effort to help him build it.

After my meeting with the King and the health minister, my

wife and I returned to Pittsburgh to close our house and to bring our children with us to Tehran. As we were planning to move back to Iran in 1979, I read in the newspapers of the fall of Mohammad Reza Shah. There had been a bloody revolution in Tehran, forcing the Shah to leave the country. This was shocking to me and totally unexpected. I had known the King as a charming and intelligent person who had great ambition to advance his country and who wanted to help it to become like the countries in Western Europe. Earlier in the 1940s when the young King replaced his father on the Persian Peacock Throne, he had immediately freed the champion of democracy, Mossadegh, who had been imprisoned by the young King's father. He also granted freedom of the press and allowed the formation of political parties. The Parliament was allowed to resume with freely elected candidates. Lastly, he agreed to make the democracy complete by putting the Iranian Army under the control of Mossadegh. I will discuss in Chapter 7 how the democracy in Iran was secretly demolished by the U.S. government.

I am sorry to say that after several thousand years of reign, the Persian Kingdom came to a bloody end in 1979 with the departure of His Majesty the Mohammad Reza Shah. I had known and respected him all my life, even with his flaws, but he was gone before I could say goodbye and wish him well. The Shah died from cancer within a year of his overthrow by angry Iranians.

I always get impressed and joyful when I read of the several thousand years of history of the Persian Kings. A large number of them made great contributions to our civilization.

My favorite King, Cyrus the Great, who lived in 600-530 BCE, built the biggest empire in the world. Cyrus did not allow the massacre of conquered people, and he respected their cultures and religions. When he captured Babylon, he freed all the Jews held captive and sent them home to Jerusalem. The prophet Isaiah called him an anointed one. The most important relic of Cyrus is his Cylinder, which is in the British Museum. It is the first proclamation of human rights, freedom of religion, equality of races, and justice for all.

6. The Islamist Takeover of Iran

After the revolution, the Iranian people brought the cleric Khomeini back from exile. Khomeini hated the Mohamed Reza Shah because he thought the Shah was not religious. Khomeini forced people to wear the chador instead of fashionable dress, and he did not allow them to drink alcohol or eat certain foods, like pork. The deceived Iranians believed that Khomeini would be a holy man—a benevolent person—who would bring back democracy and human rights, similar to what had been first achieved in 1906 with a constitutional monarchy. At that time the Iranian people had revolted against a Ghajar King and established a constitution and a parliament. Unfortunately, the people were wrong in what they imagined Khomeini would do. Khomeini did not care to be a father figure and did not like people to consider him as such. What he wanted was to become the Supreme Leader of the country and to enforce the rules of a hard-line Islamist. He executed a large number of people who were not following the rules of the Moslem religion.

The killing was so massive and thoughtless that the deputy and the right-hand man to Khomeini, Ayatollah Montazeri, resigned from his job.

The people who forced the Shah to abdicate created a miserable life for themselves. Under the Shah, they had full social freedom. They could go dancing, wear any clothing they liked,

The Revolutionary Guard massacred the Iranians who did not follow the strict rules of the Moslem religion and opposed the government.

hold hands with their loved ones, and eat any food they liked. Under the Islamists, they lost both social and political freedoms. At least under the Shah they had social freedom.

Most recently, on October 28, 2016, the birthday of King Cyrus the Great, thousands of peaceful Iranians gathered from all over the country to protest the ruthless policy of hard-line Islamists. They gathered around King Cyrus's tomb and demanded freedom, human rights, and an end to war in the Middle East. Cyrus was the first King in the world to declare human rights for all of his citizens and freedom for other peoples. He rescued the Jews from slavery and allowed them to return to Jerusalem. In sharp contrast to Cyrus, the Islamist rulers put many of the peaceful demonstrators in jail. They did not know that our important Presidents like Thomas Jefferson and Harry S. Truman were great admirers of Cyrus for his good will toward all peoples in his empire.

In late 2017, I heard on BBC Radio and read in the newspapers that there had been revolts of Iranians against their Islamic government. The Iranian people were asking for improvements in their economy, including making their food more affordable. The government responded by killing and jailing the demonstrators.

In 2016, thousands of peaceful Iranians gathered around the
tomb of King Cyrus the Great to demand human rights.

This changed the revolt for food to one demanding political
changes in their government. Their demands included change
from the religious theocracy to a democracy, removing the
supreme leader Ayatollah Ali Khamenei from the position of
power, and no longer spending Iranian money to fund other
Middle Eastern countries at war.

Iranians revolting against their government is not new. They
have done it several times in the past, but each time the revolt
has been crushed by the Revolutionary Guard, the military force
of the Islamic Republic. The Revolutionary Guard has been able to
push back the protestors by killing and jailing them. The economic
hardship and suffering continues without any solution. The *Wall
Street Journal* has speculated that the country is misusing their
funds. For example, the Islamic Revolutionary Guard is slated to
receive $8 billion to support wars in Iraq, Syria, and Yemen. And
the *New York Times* reported that the corruption of the banks, the
judiciary, and the clerical institutions have fueled the revolt of the

working class, who are losing their savings.[2] As a result, the poor people are doomed to suffer.

---

2 January 21, 2018

7. American Ousting of Mossadegh and His Government

Until the 1950s, warm and friendly relations existed between Americans and Iranians. Iranians loved President Harry Truman for his financial support and for forcing the Russian Army to return to their own country after WWII. He even said no to Winston Churchill when Churchill asked for Truman's permission to take back the Iranian oil wells. Truman told Churchill that he would like the Iranians to use their oil to improve their economy and their country.

This controversy over oil goes back to the early 20th century when the British discovered oil in Iran and pressured the ignorant Ghajar King for permission to build wells to drill the oil for export to England. In return, England shared a token amount of income with Iran. The result was that the English became rich and the Iranians remained poor.

Later in the 1940s, when Mossadegh became the Prime Minister of Iran, his major aim was to nationalize the oil and use the income to eradicate rampant poverty in his country. The British used every possible measure to stop Mossadegh. They threatened to send the Royal Navy to take over the oil wells. This action was not allowed by President Truman. He argued that Iran needs its oil wells to emerge from poverty.

The British then tried to take Mossadegh to the International Court in The Hague and to the United Nations, but each time Mossadegh won his arguments. As a result, Mossadegh became a popular man, especially among people under the colonial control of England. In 1951, *Time* magazine put Mossadegh on its cover as "Man of the Year." He was invited to the White House as the guest of President Truman.

President Truman warmly welcoming Dr. Mossadegh to the White House.

In the early 1950s, Eisenhower became the President. He chose Allen Dulles as his Secretary of State and his brother John Dulles as the director of the Central Intelligence Agency (CIA). They were both fanatical anti-communists. Churchill convinced the two Dulles brothers that Mossadegh was pro-communist. The Dulles brothers pressured Eisenhower for permission to arrest Mossadegh and his government. Eisenhower reluctantly agreed to the coup in contradiction to his warnings about the danger of a global military-industrial complex.

The brilliant CIA agent who was selected to do the covert

operation in Tehran was Kermit Roosevelt, the grandson of
Theodore Roosevelt. He packed a suitcase full of U.S. dollars to
be used to hire smart criminals to do the covert operation against
Mossadegh. But first he had to get the permission from the
King for the covert operation. The King was reluctant to give his
permission, but Roosevelt was persistent. He finally informed the
King that the President of the United States demanded permission
for the covert operation. The King realized he had no choice
because he highly respected President Eisenhower, but he did not
want to be a part of it. Roosevelt had to try several times to bring
down Mossadegh from his position as the Prime Minister. After
succeeding in completing his job, he received instruction from
Washington to instruct the King to take over the full position of his
government to free the country from the communists.

The United States, with the help of Israel, created an efficient
secret service called Savak for the Shah to try to eliminate the
communists from his land. Years later, at his abdication, the King
confessed that he had made a mistake in following the American
instruction, but it was too late to change it.

Twenty-six years after the coup, Roosevelt wrote the book
Countercoup,[3] in which he confessed that he should not have done
the covert operation against Mossadegh.

I was not aware of the covert operation until 2003, when I
read Steven Kinzer's *All the Shah's Men.*[4] I was outraged by the
American criminal action. I simply did not expect this from the
government that I highly respected. This action in 1953 was the
first hostile American action against Iran, and it has caused serious
damage.

3   Kermit Roosevelt, *Countercoup: The Struggle for the Control of Iran*, McGraw
    Hill Company, 1979
4   Kinzer, S., *All the Shah's Men: An American Coup and the Roots of Middle
    Eastern Terror*, Hoboken, NY: John Wiley and Sons, Inc., 2003

8. Khomeini's Fear of America

After the Iranian revolution of 1978, the Shah had to leave Iran because he could not withstand the bloody warfare. President Jimmy Carter invited the Shah to come to America. When Khomeini heard this, he became fearful that the Americans were planning to restore the Shah to his throne. To prevent this, he encouraged his Islamist supporters to take over the American Embassy and hold its diplomatic members as hostages. This was followed by many demonstrations, with people shouting, "Death to America." The hostage-taking and demonstrations caused a great deal of concern and anger among Americans.

After 144 days, Khomeini realized that there would be no return for the Shah, so he ordered the hostages released.

To punish the Supreme Leader and his followers, President Ronald Regan in the 1980s encouraged Saddam Hussein, the President of Iraq, to attack Iran. The war lasted for eight years. Saddam Hussein used toxic nerve gas to kill over half a million Iranians, without either side claiming a victory.

After the first American animosity, which led to the destruction of the government of Mossadegh, the second American animosity occurred during the presidency of Mohammad Khatami, who was President from 1997 to 2005. The Iranian President proposed peaceful relations between the U.S. and Iran and began to work on it. Unexpectedly, President George W. Bush, in his State of the

Union speech before the Congress, labeled Iran as part of an "Axis of Evil." This proclamation resulted in the Iranians losing interest in Khatami and his efforts to bring peace between Iran and the U.S. Such a reaction pleased the Islamists, who hated the Americans.

9. Nuclear Enrichment

In 2002, the National Council of Resistance of Iran reported that Iran had begun a program of nuclear enrichment. This report concerned me because of its possible effect on world peace. This also became a great concern to Americans and their allies, so they asked the Iranians to stop it. The Iranians responded by claiming that their plan has been to use nuclear power for peaceful purposes and not for bomb-making. The U.S. and its allies did not believe this claim. As a result, they imposed severe sanctions that caused great economic hardships and isolation.

President Barak Obama, in a speech he gave in Egypt, promised to resolve the controversy by peaceful negotiations. This brought joy to all Iranians, but unfortunately Obama's approach was criticized by the Republicans in Congress. He decided to wait until his second term.

During his second term, he asked his Secretary of State, John Kerry, to negotiate a nuclear peace accord with Iran's foreign secretary, Mohammad Zarif. This attempt was warmly supported by Iranian President Hassan Rouhani. The negotiations took over two years of heated debates between Kerry and Zarif before an agreement was finally reached. The resulting nuclear peace accord was signed by the U.S. and its allies Germany, France, Britain, Russia, and China, and also by the President of Iran. This was considered a major achievement of Obama because until then, no one had succeeded in making peace with the Iranians. The Iranians agreed to give up their enrichment program and to allow the U.S. and the United Nations agents to perform regular inspections. This was achieved in a short time. In return, the U.S. agreed to stop sanctions, give back the Iranian assets kept in the U.S. banks, and allow business transactions. The Iranians immediately asked to buy U.S. passenger planes from Boeing because they were desperately in need of them. Obama agreed. He even went further by proposing to send American experts to teach Iranians how to fly the new planes and to open an office in Tehran for cooperation.

Unfortunately, before Obama could secure his plans, Donald Trump became the President and tried to change everything his predecessor had accomplished.

10. Donald Trump's Takeover of the Government

When Donald Trump became the President in 2017, he began reversing the progress that had been made in establishing peaceful relations between the U.S. and Iran.

Trump's Dislike of the Nuclear Accord

The first move Trump made was to sharply criticize the deal with Iran. He called it the worst deal the U.S. has made and said it should be eliminated. He totally ignored the advice of a large group of scientists and Nobel Prize winners who told him that the nuclear deal with Iran is the best we could hope for. He refused to recertify the nuclear agreement, despite being urged to do so by the United Nations experts.

International Partners

Trump also paid no attention to the wishes of our international partners who wanted to do business with Iran. Therefore, the U.S. lost relations with the international business partners when Trump refused to sign the agreement. Instead, he put new sanctions in place and stopped the Iranians from getting back the bulk of their frozen assets.

Consequences of Cancelling the Nuclear Agreement

The most serious consequence of a cancellation of the nuclear accord would be that the Iranians could potentially go back to making nuclear weapons, endangering world peace.

Calling Iranians "Terrorists"

Trump accused Iranians of being terrorists, although he has no proof. On the other hand, he went to Saudi Arabia to offer them armaments, even though people from that country killed several thousand Americans in the 9/11 attack.

Trump repeatedly has said that he would like to attack Iran to destroy it. He probably does not know that Iran is a large country with a population of 80 million people and a powerful army. Therefore, if attacked, there would be a great loss of American soldiers.

Ballistic Missiles

Because Trump's claim that Iranians were terrorists had very little support, he took on the issue of the ballistic missiles that the Iranians were building. First, the ballistic missile program was not an issue brought up in the nuclear accord. Second, the Iranians were building ballistic missiles to defend their country against attack by Middle Eastern countries, such as Iraq. Iranians lost 500,000 people when Saddam Hussein attacked them. The supreme leader, Ali Khamenei, has claimed that the ballistic missiles are only for defense against other Middle Eastern countries and not for endangering world peace.

It is unfortunate that Trump is not aware of the ancient hostility between the Arabs and the Persians. His ignorance has seriously affected the conflicts in the Middle East. In the Middle Ages, the Safavid dynasty became a powerful kingdom in Persia. The King declared Shia Islam as the official religion in the kingdom. This declaration was intended to separate the Iranians from the Arabs. The Sunnis follow the way of the prophet Mohammad, who received the traditions directly from God. In contrast, the Shiites believe that the religious mission of the prophet is continued through the descendants of Ali and the 12 Imams who are his successors.

For centuries the controversy was kept dormant until George W. Bush ignited a war in the Middle East. This resulted in awakening hostilities between the two branches of Islam. The two branches of Islam are Sunni and Shiite, and they hate each other. In all of the Middle Eastern countries we have attacked, the wars are worsened by the religious differences. The Shiites, who are mostly in Iran, and Sunnis, who are mostly in Saudi Arabia, are involved in either defending an existing government or in trying to unseat one. Therefore, there is a possibility of war between them. This possibility is suggested by a recent incident in which Saudi Arabia was attacked by a ballistic missile. The attack understandably angered the rulers of Saudi Arabia, and, more dangerously, it increased their suspicion of Iran, as they believed the missile was sent from that country.

Iranian Defense

For the past 300 years, the Iranians have not attacked any country and have remained peaceful. But recently, they have become involved in Syria and Yemen, defending the Shiites and preventing them from getting killed by the Sunnis. However, if they get attacked by any country, they are likely to respond with brutal force. Such an action would unite all of the Iranians against a foreign aggressor.

World Peace

In the summer of 2006, when I was biking on Martha's Vineyard near my summer home, I was stopped by a reporter from the *Vineyard Gazette*. He asked what I was thinking while I was biking along the island's scenic roads with their pristine views on either side of ponds, ocean, rolling fields, and sandy beaches. Without any hesitation, I told him, "world peace." This was promptly published on the front page of the *Gazette* in September 2006.

Since this publication, I have become an active advocate for world peace.

Pondering peace on a bicycle in Martha's Vineyard

Anxiety About Trump's Behavior

Thus far, Trump does not appear to have the capability or the credibility to manage his government. He says things in a speech in public and then tweets something entirely different. This kind of double-talk has led to anxiety of the American people about their future. This includes anxiety about health care, tax reform, treatment of immigrants, and many other things, such as his planning warfare in Iran. Senator Bob Corker even went further to claim that Trump could take us toward World War III.[5] Lastly, he angered the European leaders by pulling out of the Paris Agreement on Climate Change, which is a high priority for saving our planet.

---

5 *New York Times*, October 8, 2017

Demonstrations Against Trump

Trump promised to make "America great again." To become prosperous, the U.S. needs the support of scientists whose research he has greatly curtailed. In fact, the scientists held a big demonstration in Washington on April 22, 2017, to tell Trump that the promise of becoming a leader in the world needs the support of the country's scientists. The National Institute of Health needs to give grants to researchers to find cures for illnesses. To advance the quality of life, scientists need to be funded so that they can continue to expand the range of discovery.

Success of Iranian-Americans

According to the *Huffington Post,* Iranians are the most successful minority group in America.[6] They have made significant contributions to our economy, science, and arts. Furthermore, they have already shown their love of America by calling the great city Los Angeles "Tehrangeles." It is therefore a disgrace that Trump has been preventing all Iranians, even educated ones, from coming to America to see their families and for business opportunities.

Bill of Rights

Recently the editorial board of the *New York Times*[7] questioned whether Trump has adequate knowledge of the "Bill of Rights," because his actions after taking office do not show it.

Declining Popularity of President Trump

Trump is misguided if he believes that he has a mandate to tear down everything that Obama created. Trump lost the popular vote by almost three million votes. Congress has not stopped him from dismantling all of the agencies that safeguard the environment and all of the American principles protecting our health and

---

6   *Huffington Post,* "Why an Iranian Travel Ban Doesn't Make Sense," August 9, 2017.
7   *New York Times,* "President Trump, Please Read the Constitution," Nov. 11, 2017

education and our reputation in the world as peacemakers. Even the two Republican President Bushes did not vote for Trump. His ratings in the polls are the lowest of any President. The *New York Times* in a recent article[8] has discussed the pros and cons of the Trump Presidency and stated the probability of impeachment if he should dismiss Special Counsel Robert Mueller.

Hostile Threats

Recently Trump has declared that he wants to rewrite the Nuclear Accord Agreement, but the Iranian Foreign Minister has told him that the agreement cannot be changed and must be followed. This raises the possibility of warfare between Iran and America. The leaders of the two countries appear to be totally ignorant of the arguments for world peace by Anatole France that made such a deep impression on me and others living in the 20th century.

Frequent Turnover of Advisors

Since his election, Trump has frequently hired and fired members that he selected for his staff and his cabinet, but whom his grew to distrust. For example, he replaced General H. R. McMaster, a well-respected and reasonable military leader who was his National Security Advisor, with John Bolton, a known war hawk. Disturbingly John Bolton has urged the President to attack Iran, which would bring turmoil and end any promise of world peace. It is obvious, after a little over one year of governing, that Trump wants to be surrounded by people who agree with him and who will follow his plans.

Hacking by Iranians

Despite all of the cybersecurity precautions, nine Iranian computer hackers, who were most likely employed by the Iran's Revolutionary Guard, were successful in stealing billions of dollars' worth of data[9] between 2014 and 2017. The criminals cannot be prosecuted, as their whereabouts are unknown. They have

---

8   Sept 31, 2017
9   *Wall Street Journal*, March 23, 2018

been accused of gaining access to valuable data from universities, private companies, and several government agencies, including the U.S. Labor Department, the United Nations, the states of Hawaii and Indiana, and the Federal Regulatory Commission, which regulates wholesale energy markets and contains sensitive details about infrastructure. Trump may use this information to strengthen the sanctions against Iran without any evidence that the sanctions will be useful.

Conclusion

Every day brings new reports detailing how Trump is taking the country in a direction that promotes world unrest, not world peace. The evidence increases with every tweet. There are a number of countries with nuclear weapons who could blow up the world.

Former Secretary of State Madeleine Albright, in a *New York Times* op-ed,[10] wrote of the signs pointing to fascism under the Trump presidency. She concluded that Americans need to work toward electing a new President and a more responsible Congress.

Shirin Ebadi, the Iranian Nobel Peace Prize winner, has recently[11] called for removing the Iranian Supreme Leader from power. Even more recently, former FBI Director James Comey stated that he believes that Trump is unfit to be President.[12]

Another world leader who is advocating for cooperation between nations is the President of France, Emmanuel Macron. On April 25, 2018, he spoke to the Joint Houses of the United States Congress and argued eloquently for working together to solve the global problems of trade, poverty, war, and man-made causes of climate change.[13] [14] He pleaded for a change in foreign policy from "America First" to a recognition of the importance of interdependence. He said that we live on a fragile planet and need to protect it. He made a strong case for not overturning the

---

10 April 8, 2018
11 *Bloomberg View,* April 5, 2018
12 *The Washington Post,* April 16, 2018
13 *The Washington Post,* April 26, 2018
14 *Pittsburgh Post Gazette,* April 26, 2018

Iranian Nuclear Accord. It is an agreement that is in place and has been signed by five other countries. We should not try to change it, but build upon it.

Epilogue

On May 8, 2018, Trump announced that the US was pulling out of the JCPOA Nuclear Accord with Iran and re-imposing sanctions. He did this despite the earlier urging of all of the Nobel Prize winner scientists and all the co-signers of the Accord who spoke strongly in favor of the Accord, which took two years of hard negotiating. It was seen as a crowning achievement of the Obama administration. It remains to be seen what will be the reactions of Europe and Iran, which at this moment are saying they will continue to honor the agreement. Trump ordered the rejection of the peace accord on the basis of a campaign promise, without taking into consideration the substantial negative consequences.

Pundits from all over the country are listing what some of the likely consequences might be:

- Iran could renew its nuclear capability and cancel inspections.
- It could strengthen the hand of Iran's hard-line Revolutionary guard, which might then feel free to attack Middle Eastern countries with a Sunni population.
- It could set back any possibility of moderate reform or regime change in Iran.
- It could weaken the power of the moderates led by Iran's President Rouhani.
- It could cause Iran's economy to weaken further.

- The US will lose its ability to protect its interests in the Middle East.
- Business deals will be cancelled that were advantageous to both Iran and the U.S. (e.g., Boeing).
- The US could lose all credibility and influence in future international negotiations.
- It will accelerate the retreat of the US from its former leadership role and will lead to its isolation.
- Withdrawal without the approval of the United Nations Security Council is in violation of the resolution. The Iranians did not violate any aspect of their end of the bargain.

In short, all of these outcomes have been alluded to as possibilities earlier in this book. I warned about the threat of war. And I warned about conflicts being stirred up between the Arab Sunnis and the Iranian Shiites. Finally, in the absence of any support from Trump and his followers, it would be desirable if the Europeans would take over the revival of world peace.

Afterword

When I moved to the United States for my medical education, I kept alive my remembrance of the writings of Anatole France, which I had read as a teenager. His thoughts on peace left an indelible mark on me, such as these words: "Universal peace will be realized, not because man will become better, but because a new order of things, a new science, new economic necessities, will impose peace."

I still believe peace is truly about that "new order of things"—it is about our continued evolution and growth as a human race. Our future as a race depends upon it.

Several years ago, a reporter from the *Vineyard Gazette* asked what I thought about while biking along the island's scenic roads (Chapter 10). Without any hesitation, I told him the truth of what was in my heart: "world peace." The story that resulted planted a seed in me, and so began my journey to write a book about my life experience and reflections about world peace.

If there is one message I can deliver, it is this: a single human being alone cannot bring about world peace. We need to gather together in vast numbers, across all continents, and make our voices loudly heard.

In our time, one individual who has spoken frequently and passionately about this desire for peace is another Frenchman I admire, Emmanuel Macron, the president of France. Macron is a leader of great impact and eloquence, and the world desperately needs more like him. In a clear criticism of President Trump and his isolationist and nationalistic policies, Macron spoke at the Paris Peace Forum in early November 2018, where he said:

"Patriotism is the exact opposite of nationalism: nationalism is a betrayal of patriotism. By pursuing our own interests first, with no regard to others', we erase the very thing that a nation holds most precious, that which gives it life and makes it great: its moral values."

Trump's actions and beliefs are antithetical to world peace. What is precious to him? He creates daily turmoil and dissent, both at home and abroad. He is no patriot. Our 45th president is an abject failure, fanning the flames of injustice and intolerance and operating without any kind of moral compass or desire to make the world a better and more peaceful place. I do believe he is the worst president in the history of the United States. My sincere hope is that he will be impeached, resign, or as a last resort does not win re-election in 2020.

At 86, I have lived through many U.S. presidencies, and I have seen presidents abuse power for their own selfish ends. As a longtime citizen of the United States and Iranian by birth, I continue to believe that all people everywhere desire peace, and they will always resist dictatorship, intolerance, and war. I hope this book about a life lived in two countries that has spanned from the beginnings of industrialism well into the technological age will provide a voice of reason and hope.

I still think every day about what I told that *Vineyard Gazette* reporter many summers ago. My hope is that you, too, will think more about it and raise your voice and support leaders who make world peace a priority.

So I will leave you with this question, which is really a call to action: What can *you* do today to make the world a more peaceful place?

Dr. Siamak Adibi
Pittsburgh
December 24, 2018

References

1. Memoirs of Sadegh Adibi, entitled *30 Years With the Reza Shah in the Army*, has been published in the Farsi language by Nashar Alborz, Tehran, Iran in the Persian calendar year 1385 (U.S. calendar year 2006).

2. Roosevelt, Kermit, *Countercoup: The Struggle for the Control of Iran*, McGraw Hill, 1979

3. Kinzer, S., *All the Shah's Men: An American Coup and the Roots of Middle Eastern Terror*, Hoboken, NY: John Wiley and Sons, Inc., 2003

About the Author

In *Trump and the Islamists: A Threat to World Peace*, Siamak Adibi, MD, PhD, calls for the resolution of conflict between Iran and the United States and laments the damage done by President Donald Trump to world peace. Dr. Adibi was born in 1932 in Iran to a family that was closely allied to the Pahlavi Dynasty. He traveled alone to the United States as an idealistic teenager to study medicine. He was attracted to the American principles of democracy and its humanitarian world leadership. This book is an autobiographical account. Dr. Adibi has a unique perspective living in both countries, being a witness to changes and his love for both the United States and Iran.

Dr. Adibi is a retired Professor of Medicine at the University of Pittsburgh. His contributions to medicine were in gastroenterology and nutrition. He has also written *My Life and the Overthrow of The Peacock Throne* (New Publishing Partners, 2015). Both books are available on Amazon. He lives in Pittsburgh with his wife, Joan, and spends summers on Martha's Vineyard. He has three children and three grandchildren.

www.ingramcontent.com/pod-product-compliance
Lightning Source LLC
Chambersburg PA
CBHW021338290326
41933CB00038B/976